DIG THIS!

How
Archaeologists
Uncover Our Past

DIG THIS!

How Archaeologists Uncover Our Past

by Michael Avi-Yonah

Runestone Press • Minneapolis

An imprint of Lerner Publishing Group

RUNESTONE PRESS • ᚱᚢᚾᛖᛋᛏᛟᚾᛖ

rune (rōōn) *n* **1 a :** one of the earliest written alphabets used in northern Europe, dating back to A.D. 200; **b :** an alphabet character believed to have magic powers; **c :** a charm; **d :** an Old Norse or Finnish poem. **2 :** a poem or incantation of mysterious significance, often carved in stone.

Thanks to Dr. Guy Gibbon, Department of Anthropology, University of Minnesota, for his help in preparing this book.

Words in **bold** type are listed in a glossary that starts on page 93.

Runestone Press
An imprint of Lerner Publishing Group
241 First Avenue North
Minneapolis, MN 55401 U.S.A.

Website address: www.lernerbooks.com

Library of Congress Cataloging-in-Publication Data

Avi-Yonah, Michael
Dig this!: how archaeologists uncover our past / by Michael Avi-Yonah.
p. cm — (Buried Worlds)
Includes index.
Summary: Discusses methods of archaeological excavation, ancient civilizations, the history of archaeology, and pioneers in the field.
ISBN 0–8225–3200–X (lib. bdg. : alk. paper)
1. Archaeology—Juvenile literature. 2. Excavations (Archaeology)—Juvenile literature. 3. Antiquities—Collection and preservation—Juvenile literature. 4. Civilization, Ancient—Juvenile literature. [1. Archaeology. 2. Excavations (Archaeology) 3. Antiquities. 4. Civilization, Ancient.]
I. Title. II. Series.
CC171.A95 1993
930.1—dc20 92–28305

Manufactured in the United States of America
3 4 5 6 7 8 – JR – 06 05 04 03 02 01

CONTENTS

SEARCH FOR THE PAST

Humans have crafted tools, weapons, clothing, cooking utensils, and many other objects for thousands of years. When these objects broke or wore out, people usually dumped them on a garbage pile and made new things. The discarded objects were often buried under more garbage or under dust, sand, or soil.

In later times, people digging in the ground found some of the objects that were thrown away long ago. The items might be kept out of curiosity. They might be given to a collector of **artifacts**—objects that are made or modified by humans. This process of discovery and preservation is a simplified example of the science called **archaeology.**

Archaeologists find, collect, study, and preserve artifacts from the past.

The word *archaeology* was first used by the Greeks more than 2,000 years ago. Its first part comes from the Greek word *archaios,* which means "ancient." The second part comes from the Greek word *logos,* which means "speech."

When historians in ancient Greece talked about the past, the discussion was called an "archaeology." Descriptions of the past are now called history, while the study of objects from the past is known as archaeology.

At one time, archaeology was considered a glorified treasure hunt—a search for valuable and interesting objects. In recent times,

Archaeologists—scientists that dig up and study ancient artifacts—carefully remove layers of earth from a site in New Mexico.

however, archaeology has developed into a respected scientific field.

The goal of most archaeological expeditions is to explore and explain ancient artifacts in an effort to understand human history. But the focus of archaeology has shifted. For example, instead of asking where and when farming developed, archaeologists now ask how and why prehistoric people began to grow crops.

Diggers uncovered this golden bowl among the ruins of Ugarit—a city in the Middle Eastern country of Syria. Ancient artisans hammered detailed designs into the gold, a soft metal that does not rust. Gold artifacts can survive even in damp soil for thousands of years.

How Artifacts Survive

Few of the objects thrown away thousands of years ago have survived. After 10 or 20 years, most objects had decomposed (broken down) and had mixed with the soil. After 100 years, almost everything had disappeared. The surviving artifacts were made of materials that could withstand harsh climates.

Damp weather quickly destroys cloth, writing paper, and wood. These materials almost never survive, except in the deserts where the climate is very dry. Objects made of gold and silver, however, last for hundreds or thousands of years, even when buried in soil. More common metals—such as iron, copper, or bronze—rust or corrode in the ground, but they usually have a better chance of being recovered than valuable gold or silver objects.

Over the centuries, people who found objects made from precious metals often melted them down to make money or jewelry. Pottery and stone objects, on the other

Stone reliefs (sculptures carved into flat rock) adorn palace walls at the ruins of Persepolis in Iran. Some kinds of stone can withstand harsh weather for hundreds of years.

When clay is fired (baked), it turns to pottery, a hard material. Ancient artisans crafted pots of many shapes and sizes and often decorated their works with a glossy coating.

This bell was made of bronze—a combination of copper and tin—in the first century A.D. Bronze objects sometimes develop a green film that slows corrosion. For this reason, many bronze artifacts can survive for centuries.

hand, are not very valuable and are not easily destroyed. For this reason, almost every archaeological site contains little gold but has large amounts of broken pottery called **potsherds.**

Without regular repair, even the strongest buildings eventually decayed. Wind and rain quickly destroyed wooden roofs, and earthquakes shattered the strongest stone walls. In addition, people

Excavations on Delos—a Greek island in the Aegean Sea—revealed the stone foundations of an ancient settlement.

altered buildings and made it difficult for archaeologists to determine when a structure was first inhabited. City dwellers tore down old buildings and put up new ones in the same places. Laborers often used stones and wooden beams from old buildings for new construction.

In ancient times, few cities had garbage collectors, so residents simply threw their trash into the street, where it decayed into the dirt of hard-packed roads. Over time, this gradual accumulation of trash raised the street level so that people walked downstairs to enter their homes. New houses were often built on top of the foundations of old houses. In the new houses, however, the ground floor was level with the street. As a result, the old ground floor lay beneath the new ground floor.

As time passed, streets continued to build up, and the process was repeated. Towns and cities rose higher and higher, forming different levels, or **strata,** of buried objects. Natural soil processes—such as erosion, weathering, and sedimentation—also help to shape the earth's strata, which accumulate even in modern cities.

Ancient cities, deeply buried tombs, and sunken ships are all places where archaeologists discover past cultures. Some of these archaeological sites were important urban areas that were abandoned or destoyed during a natural disaster or an ancient war. City dwellers who could escape often left their possessions behind. Archacologists of a later age might find these abandoned belongings.

Modern wars can lead to important archaeological discoveries. During World War II (1939–1945), bombs razed entire city

A recorder charts strata that have been identified and labeled.

blocks in London, England. But the terrible destruction left archaeologists with a unique opportunity. A team of researchers dug through the rubble in search of the remains of Londinium, a town built by the Romans around A.D. 43.

The scientists uncovered a temple dedicated to Mithras, a god worshiped by many Roman soldiers. The temple was removed and put on display before new construction covered the site.

Tombs and graves sometimes are the best sources of information about past cultures. Well-preserved bodies can give scientists clues about what people ate and how they died. In many ancient cultures, people buried their dead with charms and valuable possessions, believing the objects would be needed in the **afterlife.** These artifacts help archaeologists solve the puzzle of how people lived long ago.

Where to Dig

Archaeologists can spend years finding money to fund digs or **excavations** (the process of uncovering ancient remains). Therefore, the archaeological site must contain useful and interesting artifacts. To verify this conclusion, the archae-

An archaeologist makes a visual record of petroglyphs (rock carvings) found at a site near Taos, New Mexico.

Experts examine surface finds while surveying a site in Alaska.

ologist reads as much as possible about the history of the region.

Archaeologists survey (carefully study) prospective sites before an excavation begins. They note any mounds, foundations, walls, columns, or other visible structures.

A survey also includes collecting potsherds from the surface and keeping track of where the pieces

A surveyor uses a transit (a type of telescope) to measure the boundaries of an archaeological site in Minnesota.

An excavation team sets up a tall bipod that holds a camera. The camera can then take photographs of the excavation site from different heights.

are found. By examining the broken pottery, archaeologists can determine when people last lived on the site.

As part of the survey, archaeologists also draw maps and take photographs of the entire site. These experts explore tombs, caves, or other openings in the ground. After the survey, the archaeologist is ready to decide how and where to begin the excavation.

Many important archaeological finds are discovered accidentally. In 1940 four boys were exploring a forest near the town of Montignac in southwestern France. After find-ing a small hole in the ground, the boys scraped out a large opening with their knives and crawled through a narrow passage into a dark underground chamber.

When the boys lifted their oil lamps to look around, they were amazed to see brightly colored animals painted on the cave's white limestone walls and ceiling. Experts believe that these paintings in Lascaux Cave are authentic **prehistoric** art from an era that predates written records.

Some ruins have been located through aerial or satellite photographs, which can reveal the outlines of ancient cities. Archaeologists use the photographs as a guide when excavating old walls and foundations. Aerial and satellite photography has helped to locate Roman palaces and villas, ancient roads and fields, and prehistoric burial mounds and fortifications.

Oil-drilling rigs have provided another means of investigating the strata of an archaeological site. A drill is used to sample the soil and to determine its composition at different depths. After workers re-move the drill, a camera and a flashlight can be lowered into the hole to take underground photographs. Archaeologists have discovered many tombs by using this method.

Organizing a Dig

Many preliminary arrangements are necessary before a dig can begin. Archaeologists need to get permission from the landowner

Prehistoric peoples used black, yellow, and red paints to create this image of a horse in Lascaux Cave near Montignac, France.

—whether a government or an individual—to excavate the site.

Archaeologists must also schedule time for the work. The local climate usually determines the months that are most suitable. In hot regions, like deserts, winter is the best time to work because temperatures are cool. In rainy areas, spring or autumn may be chosen because rainfall levels are low.

Fifty years ago, a handful of experts and several hundred diggers were needed to excavate large sites. Untrained workers often labored under supervisors who were not familiar with scientific archaeological methods. At that time, workers quickly searched a site, looking only for large artifacts. Today, however, teams of skilled diggers and experts probe the strata slowly and meticulously, searching for buried clues to the past.

Excavations require experts and workers who are skilled in many different areas. A surveyor diagrams the work as it progresses. A photographer takes pictures of the ruins and of any interesting objects that the dig reveals. Registrars record exact information about everything that is found.

A restorer preserves and reconstructs very delicate or valuable objects that are partly decomposed

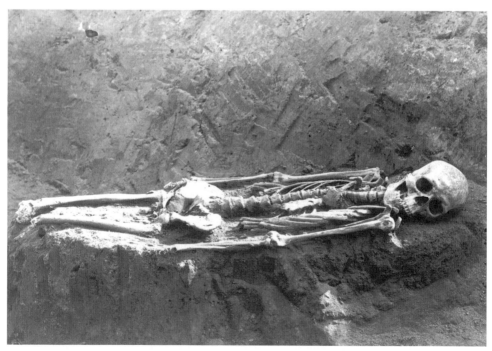

Archaeologists sometimes find the remains of humans. Physical anthropologists—scientists who specialize in the study of human evolution—may examine the skeletons to determine ethnic background, age at death, and cause of death.

As excavators carefully uncover the weapons and tools used by prehistoric peoples (below), *a recorder* (right) *notes the exact location of each artifact.*

and in need of special treatment. A language expert deciphers inscriptions on ancient artifacts. A physical anthropologist studies the remains of human skeletons.

Natural scientists — such as geologists, botanists, and zoologists — examine the soil, the remains of plant and animal life, and evidence of the past climates of archaeological sites. Their findings can reveal the natural environment that existed when the ruin was occupied.

In addition to a team of experts, archaeologists rely on volunteers — mainly students — to assist in searching the soil for remains. The expedition provides the volunteers with food and lodging, but it does not pay them a salary. Many student volunteers participate in digs as part of their coursework.

A digger marks an excavation unit with stakes and string.

Dividing a site into a uniform grid of excavation units helps archaeologists to accurately record the location of each artifact.

Sifting through the Evidence

The area to be excavated is marked with stakes and string in a grid of squares. Each square—called an excavation unit—is about the size of a child's sandbox. As the earth is dug away, the markers that sep- arate the units from each other are left standing. Dirt is carefully re- moved, shoveled into a basket, and carried to a dump site. Workers at a large excavation might set up con- veyor belts to transport the earth.

Before it is dumped, the dirt is carefully examined for artifacts.

While carefully scraping dirt into a shovel, an excavator searches for small objects before dumping the earth.

Excavators pass the soil through a screen made of wire mesh, so that small objects are not accidentally thrown away. When a large object is discovered—such as a skull, a cooking pot, or a tool—the archaeologist in charge usually removes it from the soil.

Dirt taken from a site is sifted through a wire screen with a strong spray of water. Diggers use this method to find small objects that otherwise may be overlooked.

TOOLS OF THE TRADE

Two hundred years ago, European art collectors dug up ancient ruins with sharp shovels in search of valuable artifacts. Today, archaeologists from all over the world recognize the importance of careful excavation. They use special tools that range in size from large tractors to tiny dental picks.

After surveyors thoroughly examine a site, excavators sometimes need heavy equipment, such as a giant tractor-shovel, to strip away the top layers of earth. Thereafter, excavators scrape and poke with hoes and hand shovels in search of evidence that humans lived on the site.

The final stages of excavation require very small, delicate tools.

When diggers reach a layer of earth that shows signs of human habitation, they use a small, pointed handpick to loosen the soil. Excavators then use a trowel—a small, flat-bladed garden tool—to scrape the loose dirt into a dustpan, which is emptied into a labeled bucket. When the bucket is full, another worker sifts the dirt through a screen to look for small objects.

When an artifact is found, experts gently clean away the dirt with dental picks and paint brushes before removing the object from the ground. In this way, archaeologists assure that each object is unearthed exactly as it was buried thousands of years ago.

A grid (left) *is placed over each excavation unit, enabling excavators to chart the location of artifacts before the objects are removed from the site* (below).

All objects collected from a certain excavation unit are put into the same basket, which is labeled with the number of the unit and the depth at which the objects were found. Materials recovered from a site are immediately recorded, bagged, and labeled. Surveyors map the locations of significant finds and label each strata. This careful process ensures that archaeologists will be able to relocate each of the thousands of objects that have been discovered.

Artifacts taken from a site are brought to a lab, where archaeologists and students can study them in detail.

METHODS
OF EXCAVATION

In recent years, archaeologists have placed great emphasis on the location of a buried artifact within a stratum. By studying the layers and items surrounding an object, archaeologists can learn about the cultures that once occupied a site. As a result, an artifact that is purposefully excavated is usually more valuable than an object that is dug up by chance.

In the early days of archaeology, workers cut long, narrow trenches across the ground to expose the strata. Although trenching has improved, it still has disadvantages. For example, trenching severely damages the upper strata, making the information about more recent parts of the ruin difficult to analyze.

Early archaeologists sometimes excavated an entire site at once. Most modern archaeologists consider this method inappropriate. Once the soil of the upper levels is completely removed, there is no way of examining the strata at a later time. As a result, present-day researchers have lost an important source of information. Modern archaeologists prefer to leave part of the site alone, so that future archaeologists can later check the strata with more advanced methods.

Level by Level

The first step in excavating a new site is to dig a narrow, vertical

24

An excavator brushes soil from a pot while leaving the artifact undisturbed. By examining the dirt—as well as the objects surrounding the pot—archaeologists may be able to determine how the container was used.

The walls of an excavation unit reveal different shades of strata. Archaeologists identify each stratum by color, texture, and content.

trench through all of the levels down to untouched soil. After examining the strata, archaeologists begin a horizontal exploration by excavating one stratum at a time. At each stratum, the excavator tries to identify the floor level — anything below it must belong to the next older stratum. As work proceeds, one part of the site will be left untouched, enabling later researchers to check the findings of each stratum.

Most excavations now also use a vertical method, in which part of the site is excavated along the side of a vertical cut. With this method, all strata are visible as the excavation proceeds, and the archaeologist is able to see any trenches or holes that were made by previous inhabitants.

Archaeologists examine many features of the strata — color, texture, artifact contents, and even the disturbance of the soil by earthworms or rodents. Scientists try to identify each stratum and to excavate the site one layer at a time.

Ideally, the strata should lay roughly parallel, one on top of the other, with the most recent strata

Excavators dig deep trenches to determine how many layers of strata exist on this site.

Archaeologists leave part of this Indian mound untouched, allowing future scientists to check the original findings.

at the top and the oldest at the bottom. By carefully following the floor or street levels of one stratum after another, the archaeologist may be able to reconstruct the history of the entire site. In practice, however, the excavation is not always this simple.

Ancient Obstacles

Ancient cities were rarely built on flat surfaces. In most cases, the earliest inhabitants constructed a palace or a temple on top of a hill. Smaller houses surrounded the high-est structure. As the city grew, other houses were built farther away from the center and therefore farther down the hill. This meant that the oldest and most important structures stood at a higher level than the newer buildings.

Sometimes, if an old city was rebuilt, its oldest dwellings remained standing next to new structures at the upper levels. Thus, within a certain stratum, buildings from two separate eras may exist side by side.

Another problem can arise when walls or foundations collapse. At the ancient city of Jericho on the

In Athens, the capital of modern Greece, the ruins of an ancient theater occupy the same stratum as modern roads and office buildings.

Israeli-occupied West Bank, for example, there was an old wall that fell into disrepair many centuries ago. The inhabitants of Jericho built a new wall on top of the foundations of the old wall, but as time passed this new wall also fell into ruins.

As the new stones fell to the ground, they landed below the older stones. The wall was gradually buried. When excavators unearthed the structure, they incorrectly assumed that newer parts of the wall were older because they were found at a deeper stratum.

Confusion also arises when archaeologists encounter foundation trenches dug by past inhabitants of a site. The simple process of shoveling the earth out of the trench and then shoveling it back in again reverses the order of the remains.

When dirt is removed from a trench, the top layer of earth is tossed to the edge of the hole. Deeper layers are tossed even farther from the edge. When the trench is filled in again around the foundation, the digger begins by tossing in dirt closest to the edge of the trench. As a result, new layers of earth end up on the bottom of the trench while older remains end up on top.

In small foundation trenches, this reversing process is easily detected. But in large and deep trenches, which may cut through several strata of accumulated material, the reversed layers can cause great confusion.

Jericho's city walls, which collapsed and were rebuilt, confused archaeologists who found newer parts of the walls at a deeper level.

DATING THE PAST

Sometimes archaeologists are not aware of the importance of a discovery until they begin examining their finds in a laboratory. Using up-to-date technology, scientists can determine the age of an artifact, even if it was made thousands of years ago. Among the newest lab techniques are dendrochronology, carbon dating, obsidian hydration, and thermoluminescence.

Dendrochronology

Within the trunks of many trees, a dark ring marks the end of each year's growth. By counting the rings, scientists can learn the age of a tree. To use dendrochronology, archaeologists must take a small sample from a living tree—a process that does not harm the tree. An approximate year is then assigned to each ring. Trees from the same geographical region experience the same weather conditions and tend to have the same distinct ring pattern. This feature enables experts to match the rings on older logs in the area to this pattern and so determine an approximate age. For example, archaeologists may be able to date the post from an early dwelling by matching the post's tree-ring pattern to sample patterns from nearby living trees.

Carbon Dating

All living organisms absorb a chemical substance called carbon 14. After plants or animals die, they no longer take in this material, and the carbon 14 begins to disintegrate at a known rate. For example, scientists know that in 5,730 years, half the carbon 14 absorbed by an organism disappears.

In the lab, archaeologists can measure the amount of carbon 14 that remains and then gauge how long ago an organism died —a process called carbon dating. Artifacts containing once-living materials—such as bone, animal hide, or plant fibers—can be dated as far back as 50,000 years. Older objects retain too little carbon 14 to be dated accurately.

A scientist carefully examines the rings of a tree sample.

A lab worker uses a computer to help analyze the results of carbon dating.

Obsidian Hydration

Rapidly cooling lava—the outpouring of melted rock from an erupting volcano—forms a hard natural glass called obsidian. Ancient people used this material to make arrowheads and scraping tools. Obsidian absorbs water, so that a very thin layer of mixed obsidian and water is created on the surface. When ancient toolmakers broke off a piece of obsidian to craft an object, such as a spearpoint, a new layer began to form on the broken surface.

Scientists have established a typical growth rate for the layers of various kinds of obsidian rock in different climatic conditions. By measuring the obsidian hydration —or thickness of the layer—experts can learn when the artifact was made.

Thermo-luminescence

Clay stores energy, which is fully released upon firing. The energy exits in the form of light that cannot be seen with the naked eye. After firing, the clay begins to store energy again at a known rate.

In a laboratory, modern scientists first reheat an excavated potsherd. By using special equipment, they then measure the amount of light released to determine the artifact's age. Experts also use thermo-luminescence to date certain kinds of soil.

Two occupation levels are visible at this site in Bath, England. The lower level contains baths built by the Romans in the second century A.D. About 1,500 years later, residents of Bath constructed meeting rooms on top of the Roman baths.

Daily Life and Disaster

In excavating a site, archaeologists often discover **occupation levels**—strata that show when the ruin was inhabited. Occupation levels are formed by an accumulation of objects that were lost or discarded by people who lived on the site during that time. But even within the same occupation level, changes made by residents can confuse archaeologists. Inhabitants might have divided rooms, blocked doors, or changed floor levels.

Sometimes the decline of an important town or city caused people to move away in search of more prosperous communities. As palaces and temples fell into ruin, very poor people who had nowhere to live sometimes moved into the abandoned buildings. These people changed or rebuilt parts of the original structure to create smaller, more comfortable rooms for themselves. Although these changes make an excavation more complicated, they are possible to detect.

Sometimes a building was unoccupied for a long period of time. In this case, archaeologists discover a natural accumulation of dust and dirt, which forms a stratum containing no human bones or artifacts. Sites often contain strata of occupation levels that alternate with levels with no remains. These obvious differences make the various strata easy to identify.

Another element that makes it easier to distinguish one stratum from another is evidence of fire, especially if it destroyed an entire community. The violent destruction of a city by fire was terrible for its inhabitants, but it is a great help to archaeologists. The layer of ashes and charred remains from the fire neatly separates the occupation levels from before and after the disaster.

Light-colored layers of volcanic ash clearly separate the strata at this site in Alaska.

ANCIENT CIVILIZATIONS OF THE MIDDLE EAST AND ASIA

Although excavations involve long hours of hard work, archaeologists focus on their goal—learning about human history through past civilizations. What made people who were once wandering hunters and gatherers decide to grow crops and build cities? How did these settlements advance to become modern civilizations? And why did some civilizations flourish while others died out?

Through excavations, archaeologists can begin to answer these questions. Bit by bit, experts can piece together the remains of entire civilizations and can learn how people lived thousands of years ago.

The first civilizations arose more than 5,000 years ago in the Middle East, a region where Africa and Asia meet. About 1,000 years later, two areas in eastern Asia and western Asia supported great civilizations. These civilizations shared several features. They farmed using irrigation, for example, and built temples to honor their gods.

Mesopotamia

Named for the Greek word meaning "between rivers," Mesopotamia is an ancient region located in southwestern Asia. At this spot, the Tigris and Euphrates rivers run southeastward through a long, wide valley to the Persian Gulf. Ancient Mesopotamia included the area that is now eastern Syria, southeastern Turkey, and most of Iraq.

The climate in this region is hot and dry, and the land is mainly desert. Thousands of years ago, however, watery swamps and fertile farmland cut between the arid plains. The region's early people drained the marshes and transported the water through canals to irrigate their farmland. These innovators created Sumer — the world's first civilization.

The Sumerians occupied southwestern Mesopotamia from about 4000 B.C. to 2300 B.C. They created the world's first cities — Uruk, Eridu, and Ur. At these sites, archaeologists have uncovered massive city walls, long streets, public buildings, and large monuments. The Sumerians built their cities around large temples, which were crowned with a stepped tower

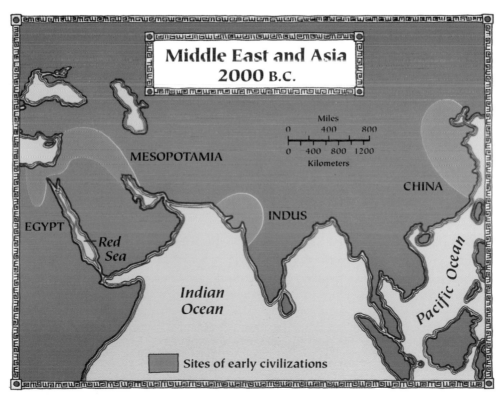

The world's first civilizations arose in Asia and northern Africa more than 5,000 years ago.

Built to symbolize mountains, ziggurats were topped with small shrines to honor the many gods of the Sumerians.

called a *ziggurat*. The temples not only served the citizens' religious needs but also acted as the administrative and economic centers of each city.

Among the ruins of Sumerian temples, archaeologists have found clay tablets that display **cuneiform** (wedge-shaped) writing. One of the oldest forms of writing in the world, cuneiform was originally used to keep records, receipts, calculations of supplies, and trade accounts. Eventually, the Sumerians expanded

This chart shows how the picture-symbols of cuneiform writing gradually evolved. Over time, scribes related cuneiform characters to sounds (far right). In this way, scholars could spell any word in the Sumerian language.

Symbol in use about 3100 B.C.	Symbol in use about 2500 B.C.	Symbol in use about 1800 B.C.	Symbol in use about 600 B.C.	SUMERIAN WORD (translation)
				SE (grain)
				KUB (mountain)
				GUD (ox)

36

This stone statue depicts Gudea, who ruled the Sumerian city-state of Lagash from 2144 to 2124 B.C. The figure is inscribed with cuneiform picture-symbols.

the use of cuneiform for literary and educational purposes. These early writings have helped modern scientists to learn how this early civilization developed economic and social structures.

Archaeologists have determined that by about 3000 B.C. Sumer's royal palaces had achieved great importance and wealth. Excava-tions of the royal tombs at Ur revealed helmets, weapons, works of art, and gold and ivory statues that depicted the life of a king in peace and war. The bodies of dozens of servants were found as well. Scientists believe that these people were executed and buried with the dead kings and queens to serve the royal families in the afterlife.

Mounted on camels, Egyptians pass the pyramids at Giza near Cairo, the capital of modern Egypt.

Egypt

One of the world's greatest civilizations arose in Egypt about 3100 B.C. A country in northeastern Africa, Egypt is famous for the Nile River that runs through its territory. Surrounded on both sides by desert, the Nile River Valley is a narrow strip of fertile land. The farmable land and fish-filled waters encouraged early Egyptians to settle in the

The ruins of the temple of Amen, an ancient Egyptian god, stand near the fertile shores of the Nile River.

TUTANKHAMEN'S TREASURE

In 1912 a U.S. archaeologist left the Valley of the Kings at Thebes, Egypt, proclaiming that the site contained no more ancient artifacts. Ten years later, on the same site, British archaeologist Howard Carter found the tomb of the pharaoh Tutankhamen. Crammed from floor to ceiling, the grave glittered with the gold of Tutankhamen's belongings.

The tomb consisted of a burial chamber and three rooms, which contained intricately carved and jeweled furniture, gold and silver bowls, ritual figures, marble vases, inscribed chests, and many other treasures. The burial chamber held three coffins. One of these coffins, made from 2,000 pounds (900 kilograms) of solid gold, held the mummy of Tutankhamen.

After three years of slow, meticulous excavation and record keeping, Carter opened the ancient king's coffin. A gold body mask—sculpted in the image of Tutankhamen more than 3,000 years ago—covered the king's remains. The pharaoh, who had inherited Egypt's throne in 1361 B.C. at the age of 9, had died before he reached the age of 20.

Carter and his team spent 10 years clearing Tutankhamen's tomb. Unlike past excavations in

Excavators discovered this gold panel on the back of Tutankhamen's throne.

the area, the archaeologists studied, cataloged, and photographed the contents of every room. Each object was placed in crates, loaded onto railroad cars, and pushed five miles (8 km) to a port on the Nile River.

Tutankhamen's fragile belongings were brought to Cairo, Egypt, where archaeologists carefully restored them. People fascinated by the lives of the ancient pharaohs can now visit the Egyptian Museum in Cairo to view the wealth of the ancient king.

area. They developed a society that placed great importance on crops and animals, using them as religious symbols.

Most archaeological evidence from ancient Egypt centers on the pharaoh (ruler) and on the royal family. The pharaohs had their bodies mummified (treated with chemicals and wrapped in strips of cloth). Egyptian officials then placed the bodies in elaborate tombs that lay in the desert bordering the Nile Valley.

The drifting sand and dry desert air preserved the tombs, which were decorated with paintings and sculptures that depicted the dead rulers as they had appeared in life.

Sculptures of royal servants and of other artifacts found in the tombs have enabled archaeologists to reconstruct the daily lives of pharaohs who lived as long as 5,000 years ago.

The Egyptian rulers sought to preserve their fame and power after death. In addition to having their bodies mummified, they made sure that their accomplishments were recorded on the walls of their tombs and temples. Between 2680 B.C. and 2400 B.C., the pharaohs built huge pyramids with false doors and hidden corridors to contain their tombs. Later, they cut tunnels and cleverly hidden entrances out of the thick stone.

A harvest scene decorates the tomb of Menna, who kept agricultural records for Pharaoh Thutmose IV during the early fourteenth century B.C. Archaeologists have learned a great deal about the early Egyptians by studying the artwork on the walls of ancient tombs.

Camel riders are dwarfed by the massive walls of a pyramid. The ancient Egyptians cut each stone by hand from nearby limestone quarries and raised the pyramid walls layer by layer.

These enormously rich rulers brought much of their wealth to the grave, believing it would be needed in the afterlife. Despite their attempts to hide their final resting places, almost every royal tomb was eventually discovered and robbed. Archaeologists will never know what valuable artifacts were once concealed in most of Egypt's royal tombs. But when the twentieth-century archaeologist Howard Carter discovered the intact tomb of Tutankhamen—a minor pharaoh—experts were astounded by the wealth it contained.

Stretching across more than one square mile (2.6 square kilometers), the ruins of Mohenjo-Daro in Pakistan include a public bath, a large granary (storage place for food), and an assembly hall.

The Indus River Valley

Ancient peoples also settled the Indus River Valley, the area that is now Pakistan and northwestern India. Like the Sumerians and Egyptians, the peoples of this region developed their society around an important river system—the Indus and its tributaries. During rainy seasons, the Indus River flooded its banks and enabled the cultivation of wheat, barley, cotton, fruit, and vegetables.

Archaeologists have uncovered more than 300 ancient cities throughout the Indus region, which thrived from about 2500 B.C. to 1900 B.C. Some cities—including Mohenjo-Daro, Harappa, Kalibangan, Chanhu-Daro, and Dhoraji—are many times larger than any other Indus cities. For this reason, archaeologists believe that the Indus civilization may have been an empire with several capital cities.

Surrounded by defensive walls, each city contained what were probably public administration buildings, religious colleges, royal palaces, and state granaries (storage places for food). Simple, red brick dwellings lined the streets, which were laid out in a carefully planned grid.

Archaeologists also discovered highly organized drainage systems beneath the cities. The streets held covered brick drains with spaces that allowed workers to clear accumulated waste. Almost every house in Mohenjo-Daro was hooked up to the city's drainage system, which contained elaborate networks of clay pipes and chutes.

Archaeologists discovered close cultural and structural ties among all the cities in the Indus region and believe the civilization was very centralized. Aside from the unique and complex architecture of their cities, little is known about these ancient people. A system of picture writing existed, but modern language experts have not been able to decipher the markings. Archaeologists attribute the rapid decline of the Indus civilization to invasions or to natural disasters, such as flooding.

Excavations at Mohenjo-Daro uncovered many small statues, incuding this animal head.

China

In about 2000 B.C., the Shang civilization emerged far east of the settlements of western Asia. Its main cities lay along the Huang (Yellow) River in northern China. The Huang

Archaeologists have unearthed many intricately carved bronze vessels from Shang settlements in northern China.

River carries great amounts of fertile silt southeastward from the highlands to China's dry plains. As a result, the Shang were able to grow staple crops, such as millet, rice, wheat, and barley.

The silt piled up rapidly, however, and often changed the course of the Huang River, an event that sometimes caused catastrophic flooding throughout the region. Archaeologists believe that some sites may still be buried beneath the silt deposited during these floods.

Most evidence of the Shang civilization comes from the excavation of three cities—Erlitou, Zhengzhou, and An-yang. Excavations at Erlitou, the oldest known Chinese city, uncovered buildings in the *hangtu*

Shang artisans were highly skilled craftspeople who used many different materials. Excavators have recovered elaborately decorated pottery (left) **and carved jade objects, such as this ceremonial weapon** *(below),* **from Shang sites.**

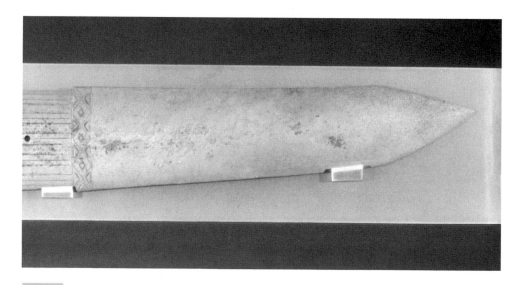

Shang warriors wore bronze helmets to protect themselves during battle with neighboring settlements.

(packed-earth) style that is typical of early Chinese cities. Carefully crafted bronze and jade artifacts were also found.

At Zhengzhou, archaeologists uncovered evidence that the royal family lived within a massive hangtu wall that also protected large ceremonial and administrative buildings. The rest of Zhengzhou's citizens lived in small farming villages outside the great wall.

At the most famous Shang site, An-yang, archaeologists unearthed a ceremonial complex, royal tombs, and a sacrificial burial ground. Large numbers of inscribed bones and tur-

tle shells were also found at An-yang. Experts believe that the Shang kings used these items to record questions to their ancestors.

The ancient Shang built a strong hierarchical (class) society with a divine king who ruled aristocrats, commoners, and slaves. Artisans of crafts—such as pottery, bronze, lacquer, jade, silk, and wool—may have belonged to a separate class. The Shang are famous for their bronze artworks, which are considered the finest remains of early Chinese civilization. These bronzes were made by a complex casting method unique to the Shang culture.

ANCIENT CIVILIZATIONS OF THE MEDITERRANEAN

In about 2000 B.C., the first European civilizations appeared on the islands and coastal areas surrounding the Mediterranean Sea. This body of water, which also borders northern Africa and the Middle East, provided easy access to other settlements.

Minoans and Mycenaeans

The Minoans, the earliest civilization of Europe, settled on Crete, a mountainous Greek island in the eastern Mediterranean Sea. The Minoans flourished between 2000 B.C. and 1400 B.C. They grew cereals, produced wine from grapes, and made olive oil from olives. These commodities enabled the Minoans to trade prosperously throughout the Mediterranean.

Richly painted and decorated, Minoan palaces housed the ruling families and served as economic and administrative centers. Food and raw materials were collected and distributed at the palaces.

Excavators uncovered large storage vessels (right) *from the Minoan palace at Knossos* (above). *The British archaeologist Arthur Evans reconstructed much of the ancient palace, replacing the crumbling columns and painting them their original deep shade of red.*

The need to keep records of these transactions led to the development of writing—first in **pictographs** (picture symbols) and later in a script known as **Linear A.** Neither writing system has been fully deciphered, but excavated tablets suggest that the markings were used for administrative purposes.

Archaeologists believe that because Crete was difficult for invading armies to overrun, the Minoans did not emphasize military practices. Most Minoan palaces, including the largest and most elaborate one at Knossos, were not fortified against attack. The Minoans kept a sizable navy, and under its protection their merchant ships traveled throughout the Mediterranean. Traders went as far as Spain, more than a thousand miles (1,600 kilometers) to the west.

The Mycenaean civilization developed on the Greek mainland southwest of present-day Athens, the capital of Greece. Mycenae culture began to take shape about 1600 B.C., and by 1400 B.C. it was a wealthy and important civilization. The Mycenaeans adopted Minoan administrative and economic systems. The Mycenaeans traded goods to surrounding settlements.

Unlike the Minoans, however, the Mycenaeans were warriors who built their dwellings on high, fortified hills. Their artisans decorated pottery with weapons and with

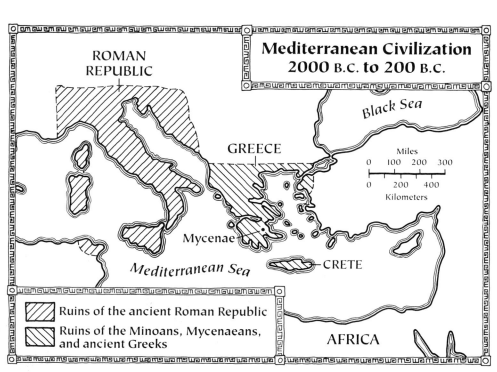

The ancient Minoans, Mycenaeans, Greeks, and Romans created busy trading routes along the Mediterranean seacoast.

Modern visitors enter the site of ancient Mycenae through the Lion Gate, a gap in the massive walls that surround the city. Just inside the gate, archaeologists discovered six tombs that contained weapons, drinking vessels, pottery, and jewelry.

scenes of warfare. Archaeologists have also uncovered Mycenaean clay tablets listing military equipment, including chariots, as inventory.

The Mycenaeans placed their dead in huge domed tombs, which were built into the sides of hills. The tombs could only be entered through long, narrow corridors. Excavations of important burial mounds reveal that Mycenaeans buried their dead with daggers, swords, helmets, and shields.

Two of the most important works of classical literature—Homer's epic poems the *Iliad* and the *Odyssey*—were set in the Mycenaean period. (Homer himself lived several centuries after Mycenaean civilization had disappeared.) At one time, scholars believed that Homer's tales were mostly the product of his own imagination and had little basis in historical fact. But the discovery and excavation of the ancient city of Troy—where the *Iliad* takes place—eventually became one of

The ruins of this Tholos—a round, domed building— stand at Delphi in central Greece. The ancient Greeks, who believed the site was sacred to the ancient god Apollo, visited oracles (prophets) at the Delphic temples to learn about the future.

the great true-adventure stories of archaeology.

Greece

People from the Greek mainland helped to develop one of the world's first alphabets. Through their trading contacts, the Greeks spread this alphabet throughout the Mediterranean region.

The increased use of writing stimulated a need for better writing materials. Heavy stone and thick clay had been the primary surfaces used for writing. Scribes needed hammers and chisels to carve the stone or sharp tools to make impressions on wet clay. These writing methods were slow, and the heavy materials were cumbersome.

Through trade, the Greeks came in contact with the Egyptians, who

Ancient Greek scribes carved inscriptions in stone to dedicate religious temples to the gods. Excavators uncovered this stone at Delphi.

wrote on papyrus — a thin, textured paper made from the papyrus plant. Egyptians made papyrus paper in long sheets that could be rolled and tied with a string. This convenient, light-weight writing material allowed more Greeks to practice writing their alphabet. As a result, many people recorded their experiences on papyrus, which could be passed easily from one generation to the next.

As written records became easier to keep, they were used in many more areas of economic activity. With the help of writing, the Greeks increased their trading network by moving from a centralized system

Artists sculpted human figures — called caryatids — to support the roof of a temple on the Acropolis in Athens.

Carved in the fifth century B.C., this sculpture (left) — entitled Discus Thrower — depicts an ancient Olympic athlete. The Parthenon (below), which stands on the Acropolis in Athens, contained many sculptures and paintings in ancient times. Built entirely of white marble, the Parthenon is 237 feet (72 meters) long, 110 feet (34 m) wide, and 60 feet (18 m) high.

The marble figures of the Terrace of the Lions guard an ancient site on the island of Delos.

of collection and distribution to one that had many trading depots throughout the Mediterranean region. As a result of this change, the Greeks became merchants and suppliers on a large scale. Evidence of advancements in shipbuilding and of the widespread use of an accepted money system also indicate an increase in Greece's commerce.

About 500 B.C., the Greeks formed a military alliance of city-states. The most important of these city-states was Athens, named for Athena, the goddess of warfare and wisdom. Athenian artisans decorated their pottery with mythological and Homeric scenes and spread this classical Greek art form throughout the Mediterranean. Sculptors carved great marble statues and created detailed **reliefs** (designs chiseled into the surface of a wall).

The most famous Athenian sculpture and architecture can be seen on the Acropolis, a high, rocky hill in the center of Athens. The Athenians built large public buildings and elaborate temples on the Acropolis. The most famous of these buildings is the Parthenon, a giant marble temple dedicated to Athena.

The Parthenon was once decorated with brightly painted pictures and statues made of ivory, gold, and marble. Many of these artifacts were destroyed in the A.D. 1700s by soldiers who crushed the marble to use as mortar. Some, however, were carried off by a British art collector in the early 1800s and are on display in London.

Rome

The Etruscans, whose origins are unknown, conquered the early peoples who lived in northwestern Italy, a southern European country that juts into the Mediterranean Sea. Their new land, Etruria, flourished between 650 B.C. and 450 B.C.

At its height, in about 500 B.C., Etruscan civilization dominated most of Italy and the nearby Mediterranean islands. Because excavators have uncovered tombs containing vast numbers of Greek vases, archaeologists believe the Etruscans were seafaring traders.

Excavators have also unearthed examples of iron, bronze, and gold artifacts. A fine black pottery called *bucchero* was unique to the Etruscans. Digs have revealed spectacular tombs containing wall paintings and intricately designed stone coffins.

About 450 B.C., the Etruscan civilization was attacked by warriors

Etruscan artisans crafted a shiny black pottery called **bucchero.**

This forum in Rome was a marketplace and meeting area for the ancient Romans.

from northern Europe and entered a period of decline. Under the Etruscan kings, however, Rome had grown from a village into a powerful city. The Romans eventually conquered the Etruscans and by 200 B.C. had built a great republic.

By the first century A.D., the Romans ruled an enormous empire that stretched from the Atlantic Ocean in the west to Mesopotamia in the east, and from present-day Germany in northern Europe to Africa's Sahara Desert in the south. Archaeologists have excavated hundreds of Roman ruins. Many more sites remain to be explored, ranging from ancient North African cities to German villas, British forts, and Roman walls.

Roman cities contained all the features of early urban centers.

Italian government officials observed the progress of diggers at Pompeii in 1785.

DISCOVERING A DISASTER

For centuries, the towns of Pompeii and Herculaneum prospered near the slopes of Mount Vesuvius, a volcano near the western coast of Italy. In A.D. 79, Mount Vesuvius erupted, burying the ancient cities in hot lava, mud, ash, and rock. Eventually hidden by soil and plants, the cities were undisturbed for nearly eighteen centuries.

In 1748 a farmer digging a well on the site of Pompeii found a buried wall. Word of the discovery eventually spread to government officials, who paid unskilled diggers to search for treasure. They uncovered a forum (marketplace), a theater, and large houses. At Herculaneum, robbers tunneled through 100 feet (30 m) of hardened lava and mud to find paintings, scrolls, and bronze and gold statues.

In 1860 the Italian archaeologist Giuseppe Fiorelli began the first systematic excavations of Pompeii and Herculaneum. Diggers came upon many hollow spaces that had formed when the bodies of the volcano's victims decayed within the hardened lava. Fiorelli developed a technique to recreate these lost remains. After filling the hollows with plaster, excavators chipped away the ash and mud, revealing the forms of people who had died more than 1,700 years ago.

By the early 1900s, archaeologists had decided to keep the ancient cities intact. Excavators have uncovered about three-fourths of the area and are still working on the site. Visitors can now wander through the ancient sites, which appear much as they did before disaster struck.

Excavations have uncovered large, open marketplaces — called **forums** — where Roman rulers held meetings. Many of the monuments and public buildings of the forums were made with mass-produced fired bricks. Permanent shops and storefronts were also a part of the Roman forum.

Ancient Romans often met at public baths, which looked like giant swimming pools surrounded by gardens and statues. The large complexes of hot and cold rooms in the baths reveal some of the advances made by the Romans. For example, the baths were covered with waterproof plaster and glazed tile and were kept warm through central-heating systems beneath the floor. The Romans also built extensive drainage systems and giant aqueducts, which controlled the supply and distribution of water.

The detailed brickwork of arches and water drains reveal the elaborate design of the ancient Roman baths.

ANCIENT CIVILIZATIONS OF THE AMERICAS

The narrow strip of land that joins North America to South America supported the first civilization in the Americas. Later civilizations arose along the mountainous western coast of South America. Like other early peoples, the inhabitants of these areas grew crops, built temples, and planned cities.

Mesoamerica

Ancient Mesoamerica—which includes the present-day countries of Mexico, Guatemala, Belize, Honduras, and El Salvador—was home to several civilizations that shared a similar culture. The earliest cultivation of maize (corn) in the Americas took place in this area. This important crop supported Mesoamericans for about 2,500 years, until Europeans arrived in the sixteenth century.

These civilizations shared several other distinctive features, including large religious and social centers and an elaborate hieroglyphic writing system. Archaeologists have uncovered numerous stone monuments carved with unique markings.

Emerging in about 1200 B.C. and thriving for 1,000 years, the

Olmec were probably the earliest Mesoamerican civilization. This culture lived in the swampy lowlands of southeastern Mexico along the Gulf of Mexico. Famous for their art, the Olmec were expert jade carvers who also created huge stone sculptures and mural paintings. The Olmec invented a precise calendar from their observations of the stars and the sun.

Archaeologists believe that the southern Mexican city of Monte Albán, which thrived from about 400 B.C. to A.D. 700, housed as many as 30,000 people. The civilization that occupied Monte Albán used irrigation to grow crops on the rugged slopes of Mexico's central plateau. The city was dominated by a ceremonial center that included temples, pyramids, a huge plaza, and burial mounds. Artifacts unearthed at this site reveal that the people of Monte Albán had extensive contact with other Mesoamerican civilizations.

Teotihuacán was a massive urban hub that thrived between 200 B.C. and A.D. 700. By 150 B.C., it

The Olmec, who were renowned stonecutters, sculpted these portraits on boulders that stand more than 10 feet (3 m) high.

stretched over 5 square miles (13 square km) and housed more than 20,000 people. Laid out in a grid system, the city was planned on an enormous scale.

In the heart of Teotihuacán stood a huge ceremonial complex that contained two great monuments—the Pyramid of the Moon and the Pyramid of the Sun. Each structure was made by hand with stones held together by a mixture of lime, sand, clay, and ground corn. Archaeologists believe that the monuments were used as religious temples, as astrological observatories, and as fortresses.

Excavators have identified parts of Teotihuacán as industrial areas where workers made tools and pot-

Giant sculptures of feathered serpents adorn the walls of the Temple of Quetzlcóatl at Teotihuacán.

The Pyramid of the Sun, which stands more than 200 feet (60 m) high, dominates the ruins of Teotihuacán.

Decorated with sculpted heads, this Mayan jar dates to about 600 B.C.

tery. The city experienced a decline in about A.D. 700 and was destroyed by fire in about A.D. 750. The religious monuments survived, however, and many cultures continued to use Teotihuacán as a ceremonial center.

The Maya settled in present-day Guatemala, Belize, southern Mexico, and small sections of El Salvador and Honduras in about 600 B.C. Imagery on early Mayan temples reveals that they had close ties with the Olmec culture. The Mayan civilization was firmly established by about A.D. 250 and flourished for about 600 more years. During this time, the Maya

Archaeologists believe that this ancient sculpture represents a Mayan corn goddess. Because the Maya depended on good harvests for survival, they often honored corn as a deity.

founded great ritual centers, such as Tikal and Uaxactún in Guatemala and Palenque in Mexico.

The Maya built immense ceremonial monuments and made artifacts from jade and obsidian (black volcanic glass). Although they were primarily an agricultural civilization, the Maya excelled in architecture and mathematics and developed a

Considered the most important Mayan ruin, the ancient city of Tikal covers more than 9 square miles (23 square km) in the rain forests of Guatemala. Two large temples (right), *which served as both administrative and religious centers, face one another across Tikal's Great Plaza.*

The Maya painted detailed pottery and murals in bright colors. This jar shows a warrior dressed for battle.

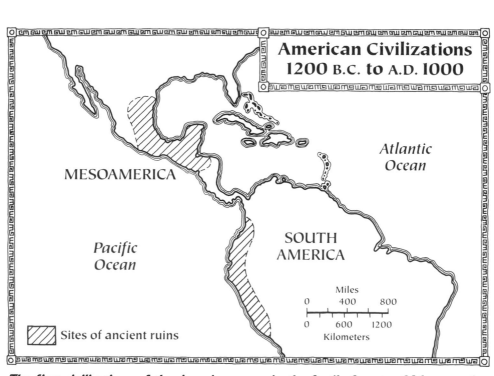

The first civilizations of the Americas arose in the fertile forests of Mesoamerica and in the coastal mountains of South America.

complex and accurate calendar. They also used a system of hieroglyphic writing, which archaeologists have found on numerous stone surfaces.

South America

Several early civilizations settled in the region of the Andes Mountains, a narrow range that stretches along the entire western coast of South America. Like other early civilizations, these cultures were agricultural, and their diet was supplemented by fish and other animals. These early cultures also developed advanced metalworking techniques.

From about 900 B.C. to 200 B.C., the Chavin art style had a great effect on the north central area of present-day Peru. Here, archaeologists have unearthed carefully worked ceramic artifacts that depict battle scenes as well as everyday life.

During the same period, a similar culture thrived in Paracas, a site in southern Peru. The Paracas people lived in adobe (heavy clay) buildings and built aqueducts to carry water from the mountains to their dry land. They were skilled at weaving and created elaborate capes in which to bury their dead. Excavators have recovered many of these garments, which were well preserved by the area's dry climate.

This large stone figure cradling a small head was crafted in northern Peru during the Chavin period. Chavin artisans often depicted two forms within one sculpture.

Archaeologists unearthed many richly decorated burial capes from a tomb in Paracas, Peru. The region's arid climate preserved the woven cloths, which were wrapped around mummies.

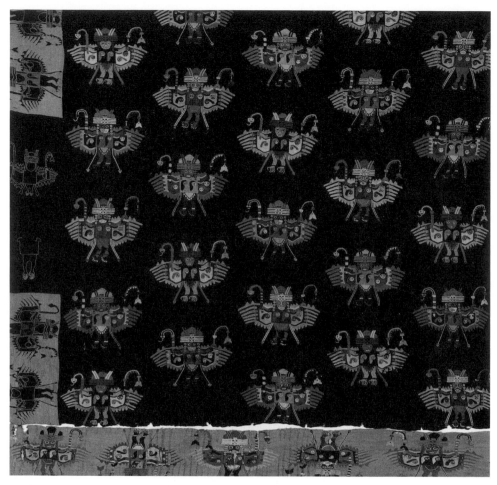

This embroidered burial cloth, which dates to about 200 B.C., was crafted in the early Nazca style.

Based on the culture of Paracas, several small city-states developed from about 200 B.C. to A.D. 600. The most important sites were Moche on the northern coast of Peru and Nazca on the southern coast. Both cities contained large ceremonial complexes that housed administrative and economic centers. Artifacts of gold, silver, and copper show that these cultures developed an advanced metalworking technology.

Between A.D. 600 and A.D. 1000, these cultures stretched inland from Peru and were gradually unified into powerful regional states. Tiahuanaco, in eastern Bolivia, was a large urban and ceremonial center that held political and religious control over a wide area. On this site, archaeologists have found stone constructions that display impressive engineering skills. The enormous gateway at Tiahuanaco—known as the Gateway of the Sun—was built with huge stones.

Archaeologists know that many other civilizations thrived throughout the ancient world. They know that smaller cities flourished among the great urban centers. Some areas have been extensively excavated, but many other sites remain. As research techniques improve, archaeologists hope to uncover additional sites in the future.

Under the supervision of an archaeologist, Bolivian workers (right) *struggle with an ancient slab. Expert stonecutters and sculptors, the ancient Tiahuanacans used wheels to position decorated slabs, such as the Gateway of the Sun* (below). *The carver of this monument used a single block of stone.*

A JOURNEY THROUGH THE AGES

In the early 1800s, archaeologists recognized that the history of almost every site could be divided into three distinct periods—the Stone Age, the Bronze Age, and the Iron Age. This theory is called the **Three Age System.** These divisions were based on the kinds of tools and weapons found at the sites.

Because different areas of the world developed at different rates, no specific dates can be applied to each period. For instance, in southwestern Asia, the Stone Age ended in about 2000 B.C. when people began making tools, weapons, and other objects from bronze. In Australia, however, indigenous (local) peoples were still using Stone-Age

materials when European explorers arrived in the A.D. 1700s.

A study of the Holy Land provides one example of how archaeologists apply the Three Age System. The Holy Land—a small territory made up of the present-day Middle Eastern countries of Israel and Jordan—borders the southeastern shores of the Mediterranean Sea. It is also a point within easy reach of Europe and Africa.

This small area is not particularly fertile. It does not have important mineral resources, and its population is low. Yet two religions —Judaism and Christianity—originated in this region, and many shrines sacred to the religion of Islam also exist there.

The Stone Age

The Holy Land's geographical position partly accounts for its importance. In prehistoric times, before the development of sailing ships, the Holy Land served as a land bridge between Africa and Asia.

During the Old Stone Age (Paleolithic period), the climate of the Holy Land was cool and rainy—not hot and dry, as it is now. Water-dependent animals, such as elephants and hippopotamuses, lived in a region that is now desert. Archaeologists have found evidence that humans also inhabited the Holy Land during this period. Most scientists believe that these prehistoric humans, who walked upright and used a variety of stone tools, came to the Holy Land from Africa.

Excavations on Mount Carmel in northern Israel have unearthed a

Decorated with stripes of red paint, this Stone-Age butter churn was crafted in about 4500 B.C.

Archaeologists in Israel unearthed a 12,000-year-old skeleton, which was wearing a headband of seashells.

group of skeletons that archaeologists cannot classify as either this prehistoric human or as modern human. All the skeletons date to the same time period, but the bodies vary greatly in size.

According to one theory, the Mount Carmel group is of mixed ancestry — the result of the intermarriage of prehistoric and modern peoples. Other experts believe that the Mount Carmel skeletons show

In prehistoric times, humans inhabited this cave on Mount Carmel in northern Israel.

that prehistoric humans and modern people were not two separate and distinct types of humans but rather were two different physical types of the same basic population. According to this theory, the modern type gradually replaced the prehistoric type.

In the Middle Stone Age (Mesolithic period), people began to build round houses and courtyards out of stone and used more advanced stone weapons for hunting. Exca-vators have uncovered more than 300 skeletons from this period in the Holy Land. Some graves held shells and animal bones, while others contained large vessels for food and drink. These finds indicate that Mesolithic people expected to need nourishment in the afterlife.

Excavated rock carvings show people hunting animals. Utensils found by archaeologists include tools with bone handles that were carved to resemble human heads

71

Some craftspeople of the past molded clay into masks. Stone-Age artisans were the first to harden clay by firing it at high temperatures.

and animals. Geometrical patterns also decorate these tools.

Gradually, the people of the Middle East began to depend less on hunting and more on agriculture for their livelihood. This transition from hunting to agriculture marks the emergence of the New Stone Age (Neolithic). Instead of wandering in search of game, people stayed in one place and grew crops.

The art of making pottery was also developed at this time. The first temples appeared, and burials became more elaborate. Neolithic people smeared the skulls of the deceased with clay, molded the clay to look as the dead did in life, and then painted and decorated the clay with shells before burial.

The Bronze Age

The prehistoric period in the Holy Land ended in about 3000 B.C. An early form of writing developed, and it was used in historical records. People lived in independent city-states and crafted bronze tools and weapons. In this period, the Holy Land was known as Canaan, and the people who lived there were called Canaanites. During the first thousand years of the Bronze Age, Canaan was independent. But after 2000 B.C., Egypt took control of Canaan. The Egyptians dominated the country for almost a thousand years.

Because each Canaanite city ruled its own territory independently, Canaan never united into a single nation. Each city, contained a fortress, one or more temples, and many small private houses. For defensive purposes, Canaanite cities were built on hills and fortified with walls and gates. One such fortified city contained large silos for storing supplies of grain.

Although the Holy Land was dominated by Egypt at this time, Mesopotamian culture also had a strong influence on the region. The Canaanites used cuneiform script—which the Mesopotamians had invented—and even a Mesopotamian language for their diplomatic correspondence. Later, Mycenaean pottery appeared in Canaan, as well as Mycenaean gold jewelry, religious statues, official seals, and metal implements.

The Iron Age

Beginning in 1200 B.C., the Holy Land was gradually taken over by the Philistines in the southwest and by the Hebrews in the north and

Ancient metalworkers crafted bronze ingots (metal shapes), which were used to buy goods. The weight of the ingot determined its worth.

Archaeologists recovered this bronze crown from the Judaean Desert in Israel.

east. The Philistines, who made weapons from iron, introduced the Iron Age in the Holy Land. The Hebrews conquered the Canaanite cities and also overcame the Philistines.

During their struggle with the Philistines, the Hebrews joined together under David, who eventually became king of a united nation called Israel. This unity was maintained under King Solomon, David's son, who ruled during the height of Israel's power.

Solomon built great fortresses as well as public works throughout the Holy Land. Archaeologists have discovered water-supply systems from this period in several cities, as well as the remains of silos and stables. In addition, a number of small pieces of pottery bearing written inscriptions show that writing was common among the Israelites.

After 538 B.C., the Persian Empire, a realm centered in present-day Iran, dominated the Middle East, including the Holy Land. Archaeologists have discovered remains of Persian buildings in the region. Coins showed that the Hebrews were allowed to mint their own money even under Persian rule.

Using the System

Before the development of the Three Age System, archaeologists had no way of defining human history. The system proved valuable in most excavations.

The Three Age System had some drawbacks, however. Dates could not be immediately determined, and some areas appeared to have skipped one or more of the stages.

Excavators had trouble deciphering the stages because of an overlap in the kinds of artifacts. For example, stone was used well into the Bronze Age, and the first metal tools could be found centuries before the Stone Age ended. The Three Age System is still a useful way of labeling developmental stages, but many archaeologists believe that a more refined system is needed.

Ancient metalworkers first obtained iron from fallen meteorites. They melted the mineral and molded it into weapons and tools, such as these iron shovels.

MAKING ARCHAEOLOGY A SCIENCE

All cultures have their own ways of explaining human existence and the surrounding world. Until the fourteenth and fifteenth centuries A.D., when a period of intellectual awakening called the Renaissance occurred in Europe, most societies were content with explanations found in religious beliefs or in myths and legends.

Art, Archaeology, and the Renaissance

During the Renaissance, scholars and artists developed a deep inter-est in the remains of ancient Rome. Artists made drawings of sculptures that decorated old buildings and of the ancient stone coffins that were visible above ground. The many copies made from these drawings helped to spread knowledge of the Roman Empire.

One of these Renaissance-era artists, Cyriacus of Ancona, trav-eled to the eastern Mediterranean in search of ruins. He copied many ancient texts during his life and made valuable drawings of many ruins that have since disappeared.

Archaeological finds during the Renaissance had a great effect on artists of that time. For example, in the first century A.D., the Roman historian Pliny wrote about a magnificent statue of Laocoön, a legendary priest of the Greek god Apollo. The statue depicts Laocoön and his two sons as they are killed by sea serpents.

According to Pliny, the statue was located in Rome in the palace of the emperor Titus. In 1506 an investigation was made of the palace ruins, and the huge statue was found exactly where Pliny had indicated.

The discovery of the statue of Laocoön created a great sensation among the artists of the Renaissance. They developed the **baroque** style of art based on the sculpture, which is vivid and full of action. Baroque art is also characterized by flowing shapes and heavy ornamentation. Baroque artists

This elaborate sculpture, which depicts sea serpents attacking the ancient priest Laocoön and his two sons, inspired the sixteenth-century baroque style of art.

strongly contrast light and shadow and emphasize depth and space. Their sculptures and paintings are large and elaborate. Baroque soon became one of the principal art styles of sixteenth- and seventeenth-century Europe.

At this early stage, archaeology was far from being an established science. The first archaeologists were amateurs who were guided to old ruins by ancient texts. Many people were simply interested in collecting ancient art.

These early enthusiasts were completely unaware of the breadth and complexity of the ancient world. In fact, almost all the ruins they found were in Rome. Early diggers—although aware of the importance of Greek civilization in the development of Roman culture—studied few authentic Greek remains.

From Amateur Sport to Serious Science

Several different events that occurred in eighteenth-century Europe helped to move archaeology

An eighteenth-century British collector loots tombs near Naples, Italy. Before archaeology became a serious science, art collectors viewed the search for ancient artifacts as a treasure hunt.

Terrified inhabitants of Pompeii, Italy, flee from the eruption of the volcano Mount Vesuvius in A.D. 79. Thousands of residents and their homes were buried under lava and volcanic ash.

from an amateur's hobby to a serious profession. In 1719 the French scholar Bernard de Montfaucon prepared several books that contained drawings and descriptions about the remains of past civilizations. Books about ancient coins began to appear later in the 1700s.

Meanwhile, wealthy English people in Britain formed societies to study early remains and hired artists to draw and paint ancient ruins. Expeditions were organized to Greece, Lebanon, and Syria, where the artists carefully recorded Greek and Roman ruins on paper and canvas. Their work—which enabled Euro-peans to see the remains of ancient Athens and other sites for the first time—represented one of the earliest permanent contributions to the new science of archaeology.

In 1764 the German scholar Johann Winckelmann published a guide to the characteristics of ancient artifacts. Winckelmann's systematic study of Greek and Roman remains and his careful analysis of the subject became the foundation for early archaeology.

The discovery of Herculaneum and Pompeii—two Roman cities that were destroyed by an eruption of the volcano Mount Vesuvius in

Mount Vesuvius towers over the excavated ruins of Pompeii.

A.D. 79—were the first large-scale excavations. Archaeologists began by digging in Herculaneum, which was discovered in 1711. Excavations began at Pompeii in 1748. Archaeologists have been working on both sites ever since.

At first, excavators were concerned only with finding items that could be removed from the site and taken to museums. They even carried away ancient **frescoes** (wall paintings made on fresh plaster) from the sides of buildings.

In time, however, archaeologists realized that by dismantling a site they were wasting an opportunity to learn about the life of an ancient community. As a result, archaeologists began to conserve and restore the finds at the site itself. Excavators left ancient shops, houses, baths, and temples exactly as they had been in the past.

Amazing Discoveries

In 1799 the French emperor Napoleon Bonaparte arrived in Egypt with his army and a number of scholars. The scholars investigated the remains of Egyptian civilization and brought their findings back to Europe. Egypt's great pyramids and temples fascinated the Europeans. Preserved by the dry climate, these massive, ancient structures towered above the desert.

While Napoleon's army was in Egypt, a French officer found a half-buried stone tablet in Rosetta, a site near the Egyptian city of Alexandria. Known as the Rosetta stone, the tablet was inscribed with a message written in Egyptian hieroglyphics, in demotic — another Egyptian language — and in ancient Greek.

Until this time, scholars had been unable to understand the ancient Egyptian languages. The three translations, however, enabled French scholar Jean-François Champollion to decipher the hieroglyphic script.

The French emperor Napoleon Bonaparte (left) *watches his soldiers unwrap a mummy found in one of the Egyptian pyramids at Giza.*

An officer in Napoleon's army discovered the Rosetta stone near Alexandria, Egypt.

The Rosetta stone helped language experts read many ancient texts and was the key to a much deeper and more extensive understanding of ancient Egyptian civilization.

During the early nineteenth century, European archaeologists traveled to Greece—which was ruled by the Turks at that time—and carried away parts of ancient Greek temples. In 1832 the Greeks gained independence from Turkish rule and chose German prince, Otto I, to become king of Greece. Otto brought with him an entire staff of scholars and archaeologists, and during the next 30 years many of the most important Greek temples were excavated and repaired.

Meanwhile, archaeologists who were investigating important sites in Mesopotamia discovered the remains of the Sumerian civilization. Many artifacts, including a number of clay tablets written in cuneiform script, were removed from their sites and taken to museums in Europe. Cuneiform writing was deciphered by the German scholar Georg Grotefend. As a result, European scholars gradually learned to understand the extensive writings of the ancient Mesopotamians.

These important discoveries encouraged scholars and scientists to develop new theories about the origin of humans. Most nineteenth-century Europeans accepted the biblical story of human creation as fact. Two hundred years earlier, an Irish priest and scholar, Archbishop James Ussher, had studied the Old Testament and had calculated the exact date of creation at 4004 B.C.

In the mid-1800s, however, archaeologists uncovered the remains of a prehistoric people that lived before 4004 B.C. Soon Charles Darwin proposed the theory of evolution. Darwin believed that humans had evolved from lower primates into modern humans over a period of thousands of years.

In the late nineteenth century, the British scholar Augustus Pitt-Rivers advanced archaeology to a true science. He created a method of systematically excavating a site and meticulously recording every detail, no matter how trivial. He emphasized the complete study of a site and the rapid publication of any findings. Pitt-Rivers's method has become the standard approach to archaeological excavation.

By the late 1800s, archaeology was a full-fledged science. Many important ancient civilizations had been discovered, and archaeologists had developed methods of excavation, reconstruction, dating, and interpretation. Archaeological findings were treated with great importance throughout the world.

Archaeological Pioneers

Although many researchers contributed to the development of early archaeology, three people — Heinrich Schliemann, Arthur Evans, and Flinders Petrie — had a significant impact on the science. These early archaeologists made great discoveries and invented methods of excavation that are still used today.

A millionaire at the age of 41, Heinrich Schliemann retired from his business in Germany and pursued an interest in the archaeology of ancient Greece. Fascinated by the civilization described in Homer's epics the *Iliad* and the *Odyssey*, Schliemann was certain that the places Homer wrote about could be located. Schliemann searched the Mediterranean and in 1871 found the ruins of the ancient city of Troy in Turkey.

Although critics condemn him for destroying many important strata in his search for the remains of Troy, Schliemann set archaeological standards for careful observation, recording of details, and quick publication of findings. In 1876 he applied his methods again after discovering the ruins of Mycenae.

The British archaeologist Arthur Evans continued the development of archaeological methods begun by Schliemann. Born to a wealthy banking family, Evans was able to finance his own archaeological research. He devoted his life to studying the ancient Minoan culture of Crete. After purchasing the land on which the Minoan capital of Knossos was located, Evans began excavating the palace of the Minoan kings in 1906. Over the

German archaeologist Heinrich Schliemann (inset) discovered the ruins of ancient Mycenae (below) in Greece.

British archaeologist Arthur Evans (center) posed with his excavation team on the Grand Staircase at the Minoan palace of Knossos.

next 35 years, his work revealed a wealth of information about this mysterious civilization.

Evans went beyond excavation. He reconstructed much of the palace, replacing wooden columns with concrete and painting them in their original deep red shade. He restored the colorful and detailed frescoes that decorated the walls of the palace. Although some archaeologists dispute the accuracy of the restoration, Knossos is one of the few sites that reveals what life might have been like for people who lived and worked in ancient times.

Flinders Petrie was a leading figure in the early development of archaeology. As a young man, Petrie was sent to Egypt to make exact measurements of the pyramids. He spent the rest of his life studying ancient Egyptian civilization. In the course of this work, he developed important methods of archaeological research.

Petrie created a strata-dating system that used potsherds. Because baked clay, the material of

ADVENTURES IN ARCHAEOLOGY

The film exploits of Indiana Jones may suggest that archaeologists are explorers, adventurers, or treasure hunters. In fact, most archaeologists rarely experience the thrill of escaping poisoned darts or of outwittting a villain. Most archaeologists work hard excavating ruins, teaching students the skills of the trade, or lending their expertise to museums.

Within archaeology, however, are many areas of study. Field archaeologists, for example, lead excavation teams in unearthing the remains of ancient people. Special types of field archaeology include underwater excavation, aerial surveying, and restoration. Some archaeologists use computer skills to compare data gathered at a site. Archaeo-physicists—who have solid backgrounds in geology and physics—determine the best places to dig by examining the surface of a site.

University archaeologists lecture in history, art, or the study of ancient cultures. Some teach excavation methods to archaeology students. Archaeologists who work in museums piece together ancient artifacts and help staff members accurately label and display the objects. Museum archaeologists provide information

Although the film character Indiana Jones encountered many adventures, his real job was teaching archaeology at a university.

that explains the historical importance of the artifacts.

Archaeologists build on the work of other scientists. Physical anthropologists, for example, study human remains. Chemists and physicists operate sophisticated laboratory equipment to determine the age of artifacts, and geologists delve into the forces that formed the earth. Through the work of skilled archaeologists, people can participate in great explorations that teach us about our past.

Flinders Petrie, a British archaeologist, applied his method of sequence dating to the study of ancient pottery.

ancient pottery, does not decay, potsherds remain unchanged for thousands of years. Since techniques used in making pottery changed over time, Petrie discovered that potsherds can reveal who occupied a site at a specific time.

Petrie also developed the technique of **sequence dating,** in which objects can be arranged in an order that shows how they gradually changed over time. He grouped pottery into many separate stages and assigned dates to them. His method helped archaeologists to trace the beginnings of Egyptian civilization.

Vast numbers of archaeological sites have been excavated throughout the world. Small villages and great cities are now regularly excavated, revealing much about the people who lived hundreds or even thousands of years ago. Through these digs, archaeology has expanded our knowledge of human history beyond the scope of anything those first enthusiastic amateurs of the Renaissance could have possibly imagined.

PRESERVING THE PAST

By studying the remains of past civilizations, archaeology makes history come alive. The Greeks are no longer just marble statues. Archaeologists have discovered a great deal about their daily lives, even down to the details of their pots and pans. The ancient Egyptians are no longer just people who made pyramids. From research, archaeologists know how they feasted, hunted, worked, and mourned their dead.

As methods of research have improved, archaeology has grown into a more exact science. New tools and techniques are now available to students of the past. For instance, the use of computers for rapid analysis of information and the development of a faster way to date artifacts have helped archaeologists to investigate their finds.

Unlike biologists or physicists, who can repeat experiments, archaeologists have one chance to evaluate their data, because the process of excavation destroys the source of their data. Although archaeologists have methods of checking their findings, they can never put a site back together and start over.

For most of human history, no written records exist. Excavations are the only available means of finding out what ancient humans were like and how they lived. For cultures that only recently introduced a writing system, archaeology stands beside oral traditions as a strong link to the past.

An archaeological team in Jerusalem, Israel, carefully probes a site for clues to the past.

Workers lift a 19-ton (17-metric-ton) statue at Abu Simbel in Egypt from the rising waters of Lake Nasser.

Endangered Artifacts

For financial, political, or geographical reasons, hundreds of sites have not been excavated. Many of them are quickly being destroyed by the construction of superhighways, oil refineries, factories, and modern buildings. Many countries, however, are now recognizing the importance of excavating ruins. As a result, many proposed building sites are tested for artifacts before construction begins.

Worsening environmental conditions endanger sites that have already been studied and excavated. For instance, after enduring for 2,500 years, the magnificent Parthenon in Athens suddenly began to fall apart. Although archaeologists reinforced the building to keep it standing, the corrosive air pollutants of modern Athens continue to eat away at the surface of the great marble structure.

Archaeologists around the world scramble to preserve what they can, but finances and the increasing industrial needs of a growing world population often hinder preservation efforts.

90

An increase in international co-operation among archaeologists is helping to save endangered sites. At Abu Simbel in Egypt, archaeologists have worked to save two temples that were threatened by the rising level of Lake Nasser.

To save the temples, an international archaeological team dismantled the structures and reassembled them in a safe location. The temples are still in danger, however, because the lake continues to rise and because saltwater gradually crumbles the ancient stone.

Military conflict also poses a great threat to remains. The powerful artillery and heavy aerial bombardment of modern warfare are far more dangerous to the ruins of ancient buildings than were the spears and arrows of the past.

Archaeologists painstakingly preserve the world's cultural heritage. They photograph and describe their findings in written records that are reproduced and made available in many libraries and research institutions. Through these and other archaeological methods, the full scope of human history — from the grand battles to the trivial details — will be within reach of future generations.

Restoration workers quickly remove the earth surrounding a temple at Abu Simbel.

PRONUNCIATION GUIDE

Abu Simbel (AH-boo SIHM-buhl)

Cairo (KY-roh)

Canaan (KAY-nuhn)

Chavin (chuh-VEEN)

Crete (KREET)

Giza (GEE-zuh)

Herculaneum (her-kyah-LAY-nee-uhm)

Huang (HWANG)

Knossos (kuh-NAHS-uhs)

Lascaux (lah-SKOH)

Mycenae (my-SEE-nee)

Pompeii (PAHM-pay)

Schliemann (SHLEE-mahn)

Sumer (SOO-muhr)

Teotihuacán (tay-oh-tee-wuh-KAHN)

Tiahuanaco (tee-uh-wuh-NAHK-oh)

Tutankhamen (too-tan-KAHM-uhn)

Uaxactún (wash-ahk-TOON)

Excavators wave from a site in southwestern Minnesota.

GLOSSARY

afterlife: an existence after death.

archaeology: the scientific study of the material remains of past human life.

artifact: any object made by a human. Artifacts can include items crafted from natural materials, such as bone, stone, clay, or wood.

baroque: a seventeenth-century art style that features curved shapes and elaborate designs.

cuneiform: a form of wedge-shaped writing first used by the ancient Sumerians of Mesopotamia (modern Iraq).

excavate: to dig out and remove objects from an archaeological site.

forum: the public square of an ancient Roman city.

fresco: a painting made on wet plaster with water-based paints.

Linear A: a form of writing used on the Greek island of Crete from the eighteenth to the fifteenth centuries B.C.

occupation level: a stratum that contains material evidence of the humans that once lived on it.

pictograph: an ancient drawing painted on a rock or a stone wall. Each picture stood for a word or a sound.

A worker measures the depth of an excavation unit.

potsherd: a piece of broken pottery. Potsherds are common on archaeological sites.

prehistoric: the period of time before the existence of written history.

relief: a carved image that comes out of a flat surface, such as a wall.

sequence dating: a method of determining the order in which different versions of a certain object were made or used over a long span of time.

stratum: a separate layer of earth or sediment on an archaeological site that may contain ancient artifacts or human remains.

Three Age System: a method used to divide into time periods the history of an archaeological site. Archaeologists classify artifacts into the Stone Age, the Bronze Age, and the Iron Age.

INDEX

Recently restored, the ancient Grand Theater in Ephesus, Turkey, hosts an international folk festival every year.

Photo Acknowledgments

pp. 2, 13 (bottom), 14, 17 (top and bottom), 20 (top and bottom), 22 (top and bottom), 23, 25 (top), Minnesota Historical Society; pp. 7 (top), 11, 12, 13 (top), 93, Bureau of Land Management; p. 7 (bottom), Hirmer Photo Archive; pp. 8, 9 (left), 15, 19, 37, 39, 40, 52 (bottom), 53, 60 (bottom), 61, 67 (top and bottom), 70 (top and bottom), 71, 72, 73, 74, 75, 77, 82, 84 (inset), 87, Independent Picture Service; pp. 9 (right), 43 (bottom), Smithsonian Institution; pp. 10, 28, 47 (top and bottom), 49, Meredith Pillon/ Greek National Tourist Organization; p. 16, The Cincinnati Historical Society; pp. 18, 25 (bottom), 33, National Park Service, Alaska Regional Office; p. 21, Wyndeth Davis/National Park Service, Alaska Regional Office; pp. 26, 27, 92, Wilford Archaeology Laboratory, University of Minnesota; pp. 29, 50, 55, 80, 84, 89, Minneapolis Public Library and Information Center; p. 30, University of Arizona Tree Ring Laboratory; p. 31, Rosenstiel School of Marine and Atmospheric Science, Tritium Laboratory; p. 32, Theresa Early; pp. 35, 36 (bottom), 48, 64, Laura Westlund; pp. 36 (top), 69, Jerusalem Publishing House; pp. 38 (top and bottom), 91, Eliot Elisofon Archives, National Museum of African Art, Smithsonian Institution; pp. 41, 51 (bottom), Drs. A. A. M. van der Heyden, Naarden, The Netherlands; pp. 42, 43 (top), Embassy of Pakistan; pp. 44 (top and bottom), 45, Nelson Atkins-Museum of Art; p. 51 (top), Ioannis Epaminondas; p. 52 (top), Terme Museum, Rome; pp. 54, 57, Italian Government Travel Office (ENIT); p. 56, Historic Urban Plans; pp. 59, 60 (top), Mexican National Tourist Council; pp. 62 (top), 65 (bottom), Museum of Modern Art of Latin America; p. 62 (bottom), Dr. Roma Hoff; p. 63, Stuart Rome; p. 65 (top), Tom Trow; p. 66, Museum of Fine Arts, Boston; p. 78, Virginia State Library and Archives; p. 79, The Mansell Collection; p. 81, The Bettmann Archive; p. 85, Ashmolean Museum, University of Oxford; p. 86, Hollywood Book and Poster; p. 90, UNESCO/Nenadorie; p. 95, Turkish Culture and Information Office.

Cover photographs: Stuart Rome (front) and Israel Ministry of Tourism (back).